YOU MATTER

Welcome to the first edition of Thinking Strong and Feeling Smart. This graphic workbook is for primary school-aged children and their teachers, carers or therapists to inspire self-awareness and facilitate the exploration of emotional intelligence, self-regulation techniques and a growth mindset. Each piece of art has been lovingly created by author/illustrator Heather J. Ray, founder of My Wellbeing School, with over fifteen years of experience teaching adults and children mindfulness, meditation and wellbeing principles.

For more helpful resources and wellbeing education visit www.mywellbeingschool.com

Text and illustrations Copyright 2022. Published by My Wellbeing School

In This Space

YOU ARE RESPECTED
YOU HAVE A VOICE
YOU ARE VALUED
YOU ARE SMART
YOU ARE LOVED
YOU BELONG

DRAW OR WRITE YOUR ANSWER

MY SAFE SPACE LOOKS LIKE

MY SAFE SPACE FEELS LIKE

MY SAFE SPACE SOUNDS LIKE

I AM

ENOUGH · GRATEFUL · IMPORTANT · BRAVE · KIND · OPEN · CALM · UNIQUE · LOVING · SMART

DRAW OR WRITE YOUR POSITIVE QUALITIES

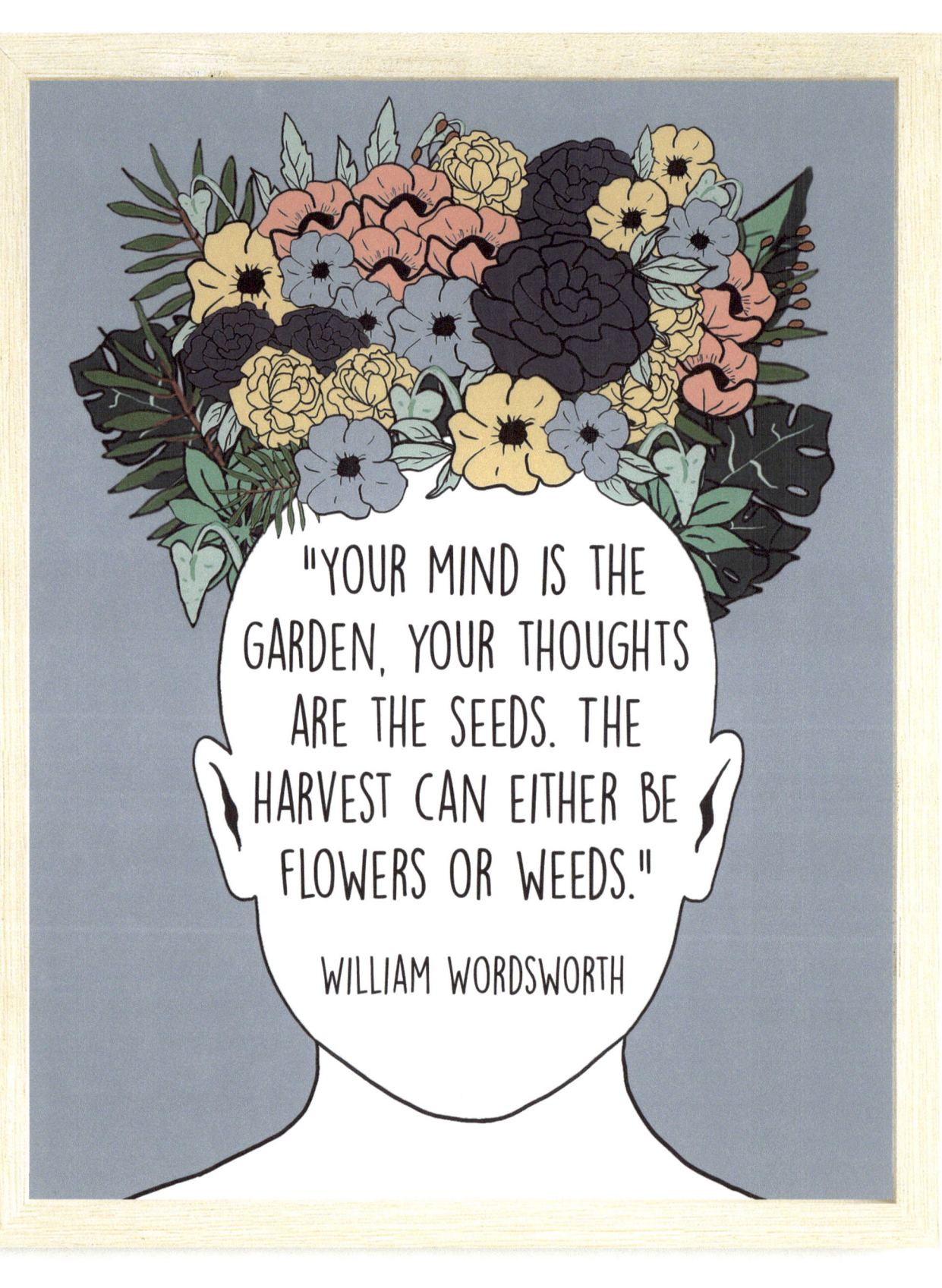

WHAT POSITIVE THOUGHTS DO YOU WANT TO GROW?

SAY YOUR MINDSET MANTRA OUT LOUD 3XA DAY

> EVERY DAY IN EVERY WAY I'M GETTING STRONGER AND SMARTER

I AM NOT GOOD AT _____ YET

I WILL GET BETTER BY _____

MY REWARD FOR REACHING MY GOAL IS

_____

(IT'S GOOD FOR YOUR MINDSET TO CELEBRATE)

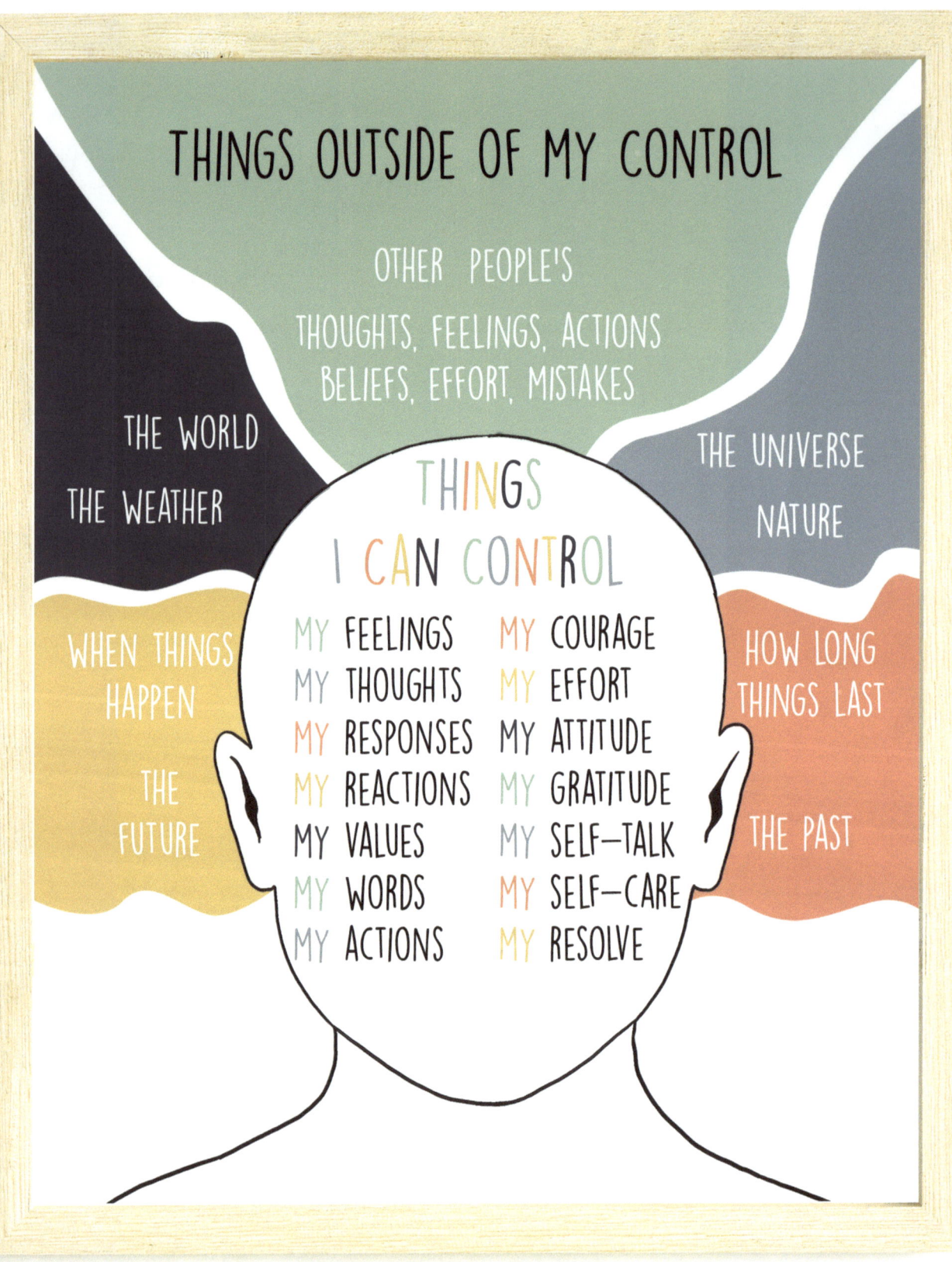

WRITE OR DRAW EXAMPLES FROM YOUR LIFE

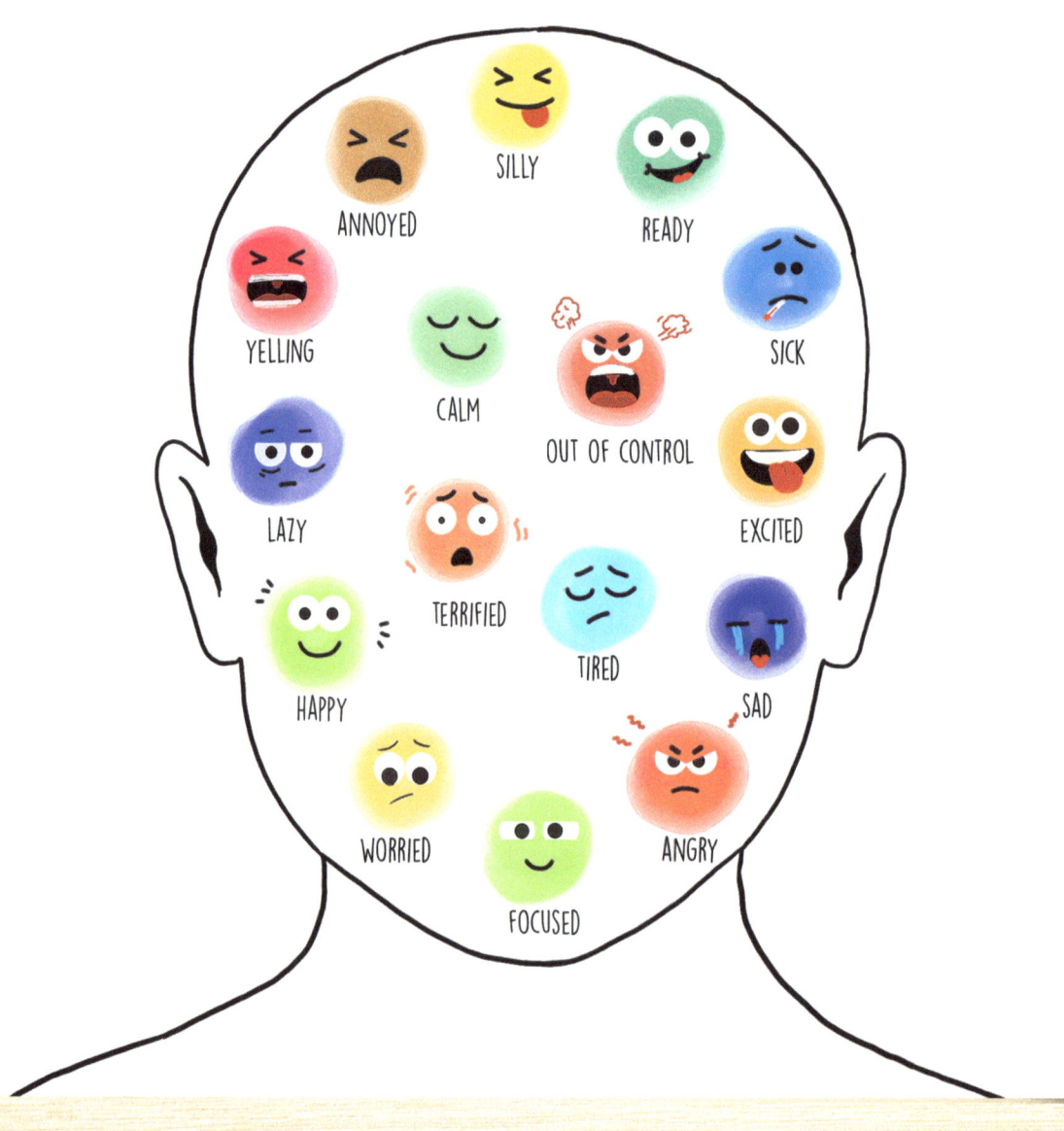

HOW ARE YOU FEELING TODAY?

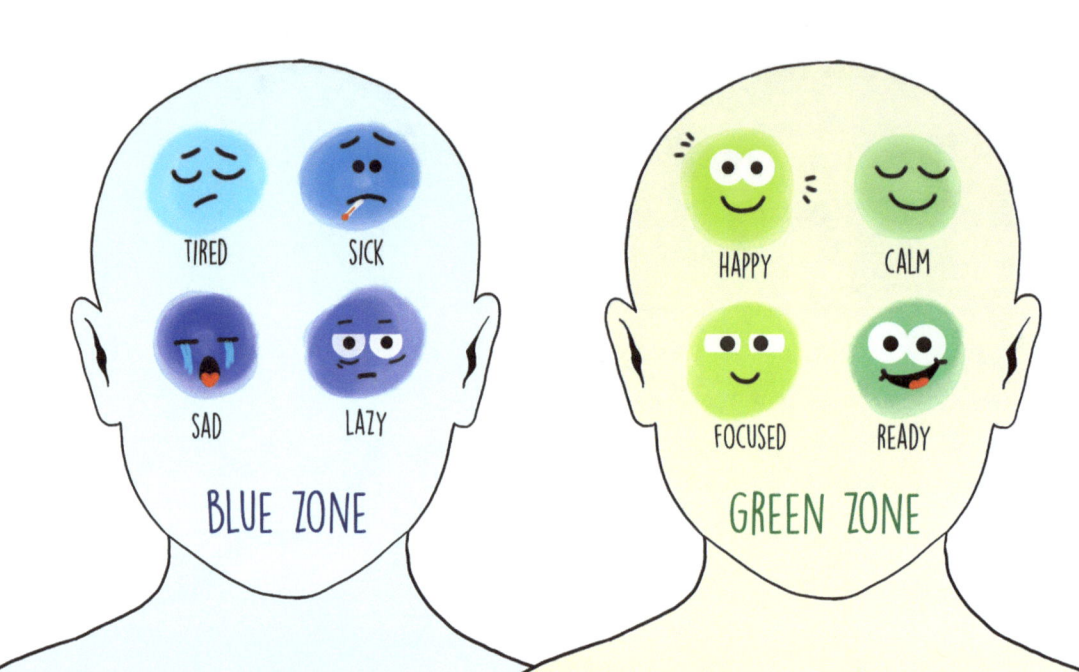
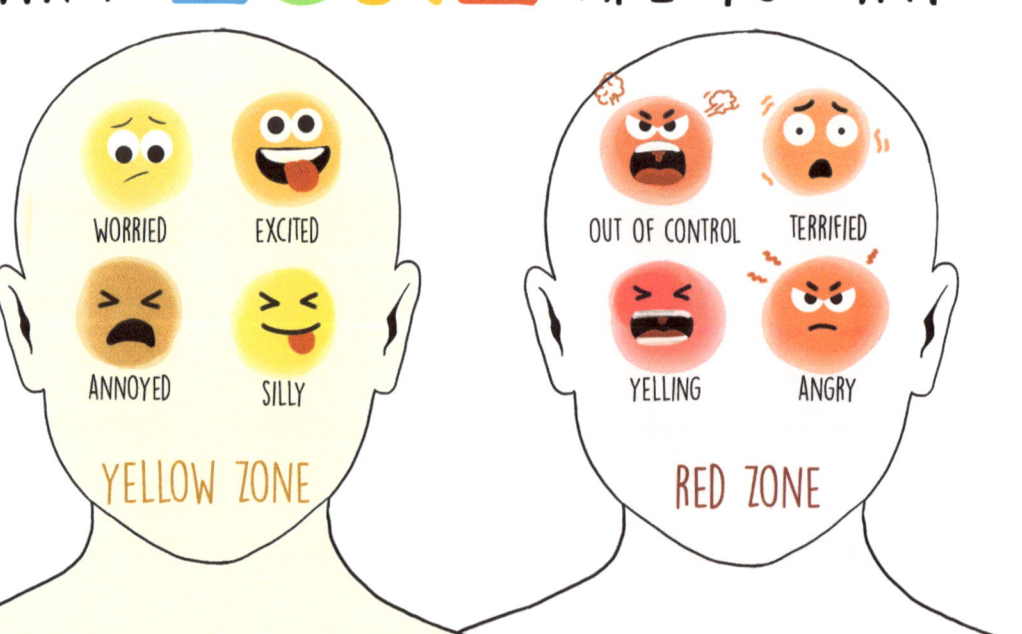

WHAT ZONE ARE YOU IN?

WHAT ZONE IS YOUR FAVOURITE?

DRAW HOW YOU ARE FEELING AND WRITE AS MANY WORDS AS YOU CAN TO DESCRIBE YOUR FEELINGS

WORKING THROUGH MY FEELINGS

STOP  Take some deep breaths, feel and name the emotion.

THINK  What is this feeling trying to tell me? What is the problem and what are my options?

GO  Take action, focus on a solution. It's ok to feel mixed emotions.

DRAW OR WRITE YOUR ANSWERS

 WHAT HELPS YOU TO STOP?

 WHAT HELPS YOU TO THINK CLEARLY?

 WHAT HELPS YOU TO FEEL BETTER?

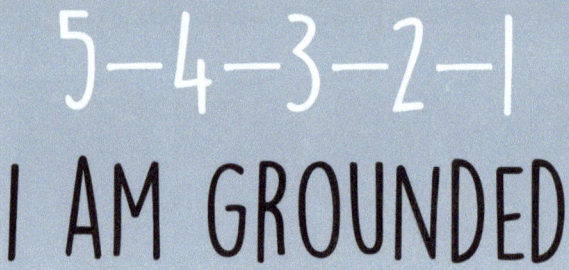

DRAW OR WRITE YOUR ANSWERS

 WHAT 5 THINGS CAN YOU SEE?

 WHAT 4 THINGS CAN YOU FEEL?

 WHAT 3 THINGS CAN YOU HEAR?

 WHAT 2 THINGS CAN YOU SMELL?

 WHAT 1 THING CAN YOU TASTE?

CALM DOWN

START

BREATHE IN

SPOT THIS COLOUR

BREATHE IN

SPOT THIS COLOUR

RAINBOW BREATH

SPOT THIS COLOUR

BREATHE OUT

SPOT THIS COLOUR

BREATHE OUT

ABOUT HEATHER JESSE RAY

Heather Ray is an author/illustrator and wellbeing program designer. Heather studied Theatre and Applied Education at the Royal Central School of Speech and Drama, where her taste for education took off. She later qualified as a Body Control Pilates Instructor and moved to Hong Kong to study Chinese Kung Fu and co-founded a Health and Wellbeing Club in the City Centre in 2008. In 2013 Heather moved to Cyprus to study psychotherapy and meditation with a spiritual group called the Researchers of Truth. There her work became more focused on counselling, healing and meditation. In 2017 Heather moved to Australia, where she now calls home and founded My Wellbeing School, a company that designs wellbeing programs for schools. Heather's flare for creativity, design, wealth of wellbeing expertise and relatable character makes her programs engaging and irresistible to families, schools and therapists alike.

MORE BOOKS BY H. J. RAY

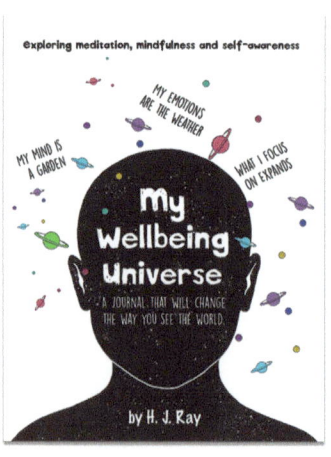

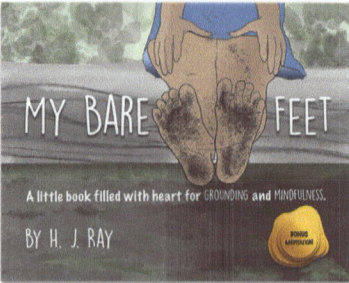

www.ingramcontent.com/pod-product-compliance
Lightning Source LLC
Chambersburg PA
CBHW041431010526
44107CB00046B/1570